The Three Orbits of John Glenn

by Karen Stamfil

illustrated by John Anthony Dollar

Printed in the United States of America

ISBN 0-15-319668-8

Ordering Options
ISBN 0-15-317074-3 (Grade 6 Collection)
ISBN 0-15-319758-7 (package of 5)

3 4 5 6 7 8 9 10 179 2003 2002 2001

In October 1998, at the age of seventy-seven, John Glenn became the oldest person ever to leave planet Earth. The senator from Ohio was part of the crew of the space shuttle *Discovery*. His mission was to test how well a person his age could perform in space flight.

Glenn performed splendidly, but that was no surprise. Space travel was nothing new to him. And *Discovery*'s high-tech facilities were far more comfortable than those he'd had on his previous trip.

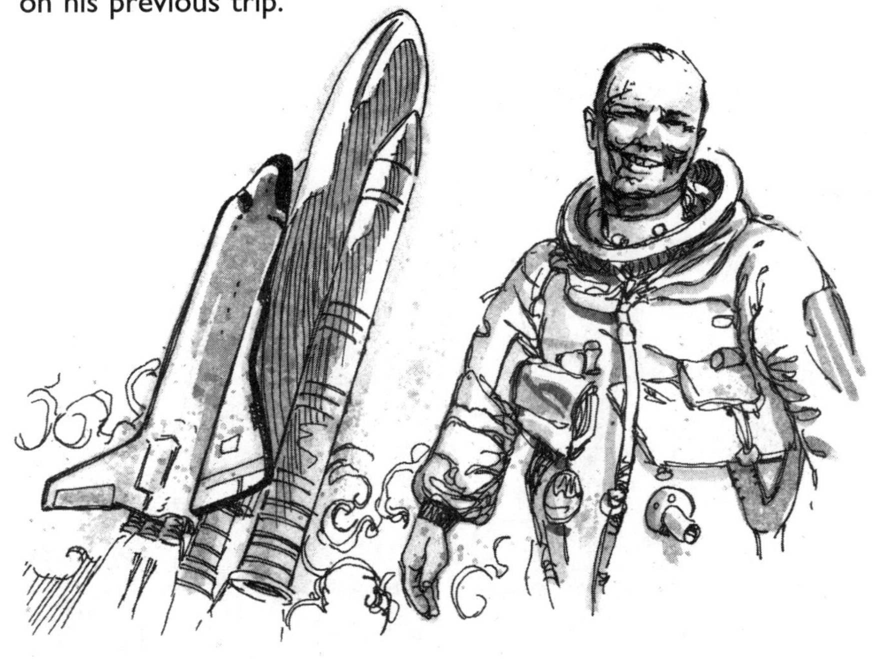

Cape Canaveral, Florida, February 20, 1962. John Glenn is about to become the first American to orbit the Earth. It is 9:47 A.M. Glenn's fellow astronaut Alan Shepard counts down: "Three, two, one, *zero*!"

The engines fire. The rocket lifts off the ground. Through the window of his *Friendship 7* space capsule, Glenn sees the horizon turning.

The rocket accelerates. It bursts out of the atmosphere. Glenn is pressed back into his seat. He now weighs nearly 1,000 pounds. He has experienced this feeling many times during flight simulation.

Nearly five minutes into the flight, the capsule separates from the rocket. For a moment Glenn feels as if he's been shot forward. Then he feels himself lifted out of his seat. "Zero g,[1] and I feel fine," he reports.

Friendship 7 turns 180 degrees. Glenn is now facing backward as he orbits the Earth. He tests the system for controlling the ship's position. He can either let it be set automatically or maneuver *Friendship 7* himself. This will be vital at the end of the flight. The capsule must be in the correct position when it reenters the atmosphere, or Glenn will not get home.

---

[1]**zero g** "zero gravity": weightlessness

Glenn's speed in orbit is nearly five miles a second. Eighteen minutes into the flight, *Friendship* 7 approaches the coast of Africa.

Glenn runs medical tests and experiments. He reports to a tracking station in the Canary Islands. These stations are placed around the Earth so that Glenn will never be out of contact while in orbit.

Forty minutes into the flight, Glenn sees the sun set over the Indian Ocean. It seems to melt into a bright white band and spread out over the horizon. The strip of light grows darker and smaller. Then it fades out completely.

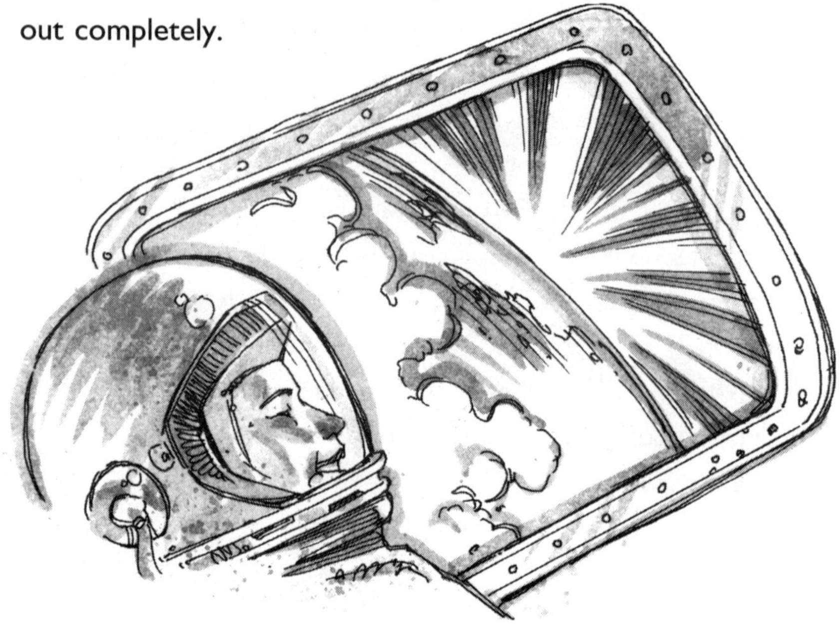

Glenn is now on the night side of Earth. He takes out a star navigation device. This is not high-tech equipment. It is a simple star chart with a plastic slide over it. He lines up the slide with a time scale. This shows him the stars he should be seeing.

There they are. That's the constellation Aries at the top of the window. Astronauts will be able to find their position by star navigation, just as oceangoing sailors do.

At NASA's[2] mission control facilities, Glenn's orbit is tracked on a map. As he passes over Perth, Australia, the people of the city turn on their lights as a signal to him. They will do so again thirty-six years later.

Glenn runs more tests. He eats from a squeeze tube. Behind him, the sun comes up. He is over the Pacific Ocean, an hour and a quarter into the flight. He passes over Mexico, nearing the end of his first orbit.

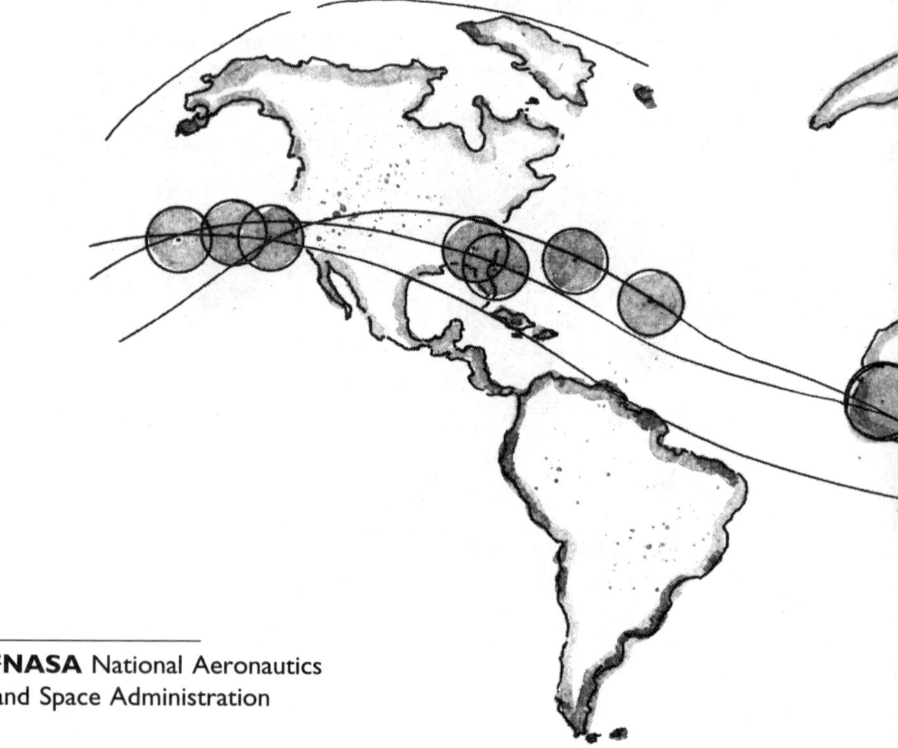

[2]**NASA** National Aeronautics and Space Administration

Meanwhile, NASA engineers are worried. A radio signal seems to show that *Friendship 7*'s landing bag has dropped into position. This is not supposed to happen until just before landing. The bag acts as a cushion when the capsule lands in the ocean. If the signal is correct, it means that the heat shield is loose, too.

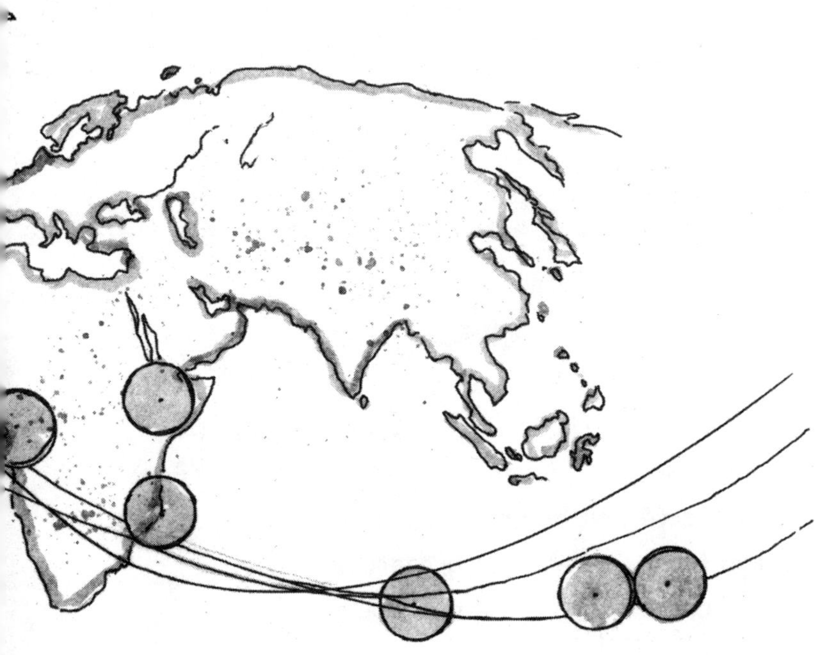

In space, Glenn finishes his first orbit. He passes back over the Atlantic toward Africa again.

Halfway through his second orbit, Glenn is told of the possible problem with the landing bag. He has had no sign that the bag is down, but he grasps the problem at once. If the heat shield is loose, it cannot protect him from the blazing heat of reentry into the atmosphere.

More than three hours into the flight now. Glenn passes over the United States for the second time and begins his third and last orbit.

"I can see the whole state of Florida, just laid out like a map," he reports. "It's beautiful." He takes photographs with several types of cameras. He passes again into night and then back into daylight for the last time.

The automatic control system has not worked well since the beginning of the flight. Glenn can maneuver the capsule back into the correct position, but it keeps swinging back to the right.

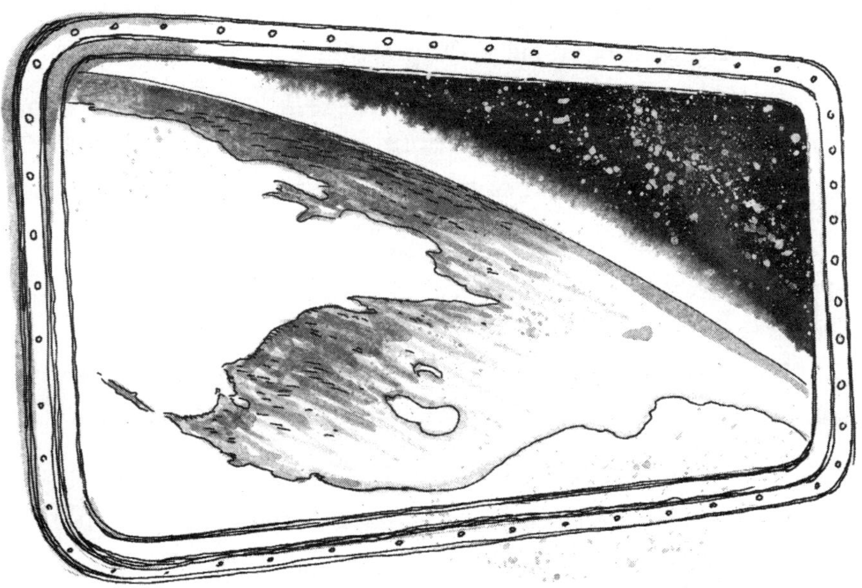

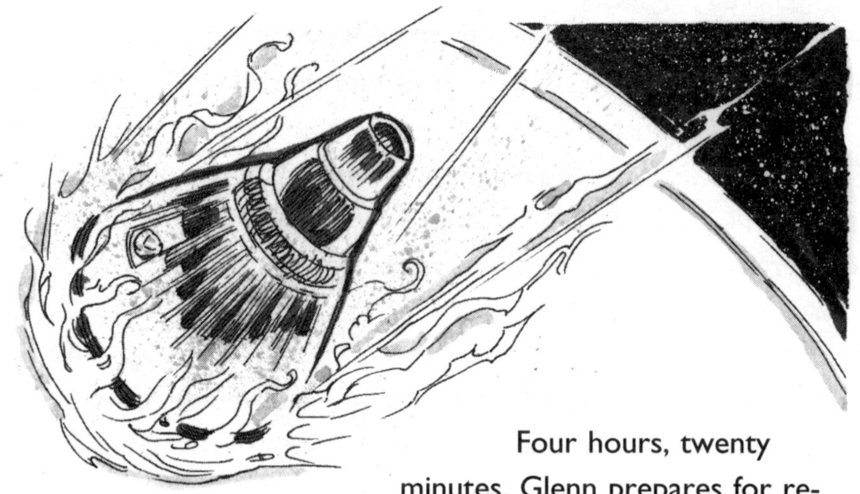

Four hours, twenty minutes. Glenn prepares for reentry. After more tests, it is decided that the landing bag signal must have been false. But no one is sure.

Four hours, thirty-three minutes. Glenn fires *Friendship 7*'s retrorockets[3]. They slow the capsule down and break it out of orbit. Glenn keeps it in position by hand control. He brings it level with the Earth.

Four hours, forty-three minutes. Communication with Earth is broken briefly while *Friendship 7* enters the atmosphere. Through the window Glenn sees a brilliant orange glow. No simulation could have prepared him for this. Friction is heating the capsule to 3,000°F.

---

[3]**retro** reverse

Flaming pieces of metal rush past the window. Is it the burned-out retrorockets? Or is it the heat shield? Is the capsule itself beginning to burn up?

"This is *Friendship* 7. A real fireball outside." But Glenn sounds cool as communication is restored, and he talks with Cape Canaveral. He drops below 100,000 feet, back into the atmosphere.

Four hours, forty-nine minutes. Ten thousand feet. The main parachute opens. It is hot inside the capsule, but now vents open and fresh air comes in from outside.

Friendship 7 slows down to a safe landing speed.

Four hours, fifty-five minutes. *Friendship 7* splashes down in the Atlantic. The recovery ship has sighted it. Minutes later the ship is alongside.

Glenn feels the capsule rubbing against the side of the ship. He feels it lifted into the air. There is a bump. Glenn warns the crew to stand clear. He blows the door off the capsule with explosive bolts.

Sailors reach in to help him out. John Glenn stands on the deck of the ship, back on planet Earth.

Ask an Astronaut

Suppose you could ask John Glenn one question about his spaceflight experience. What would your question be? Write it on a sheet of paper.

School-Home Connection Listen as your child reads this book aloud. Many people have called John Glenn a hero. What are your child's thoughts and your own about what makes a person heroic?

TAKE-HOME BOOK

Times of Discovery

Use with “I Want to Be an Astronaut.”

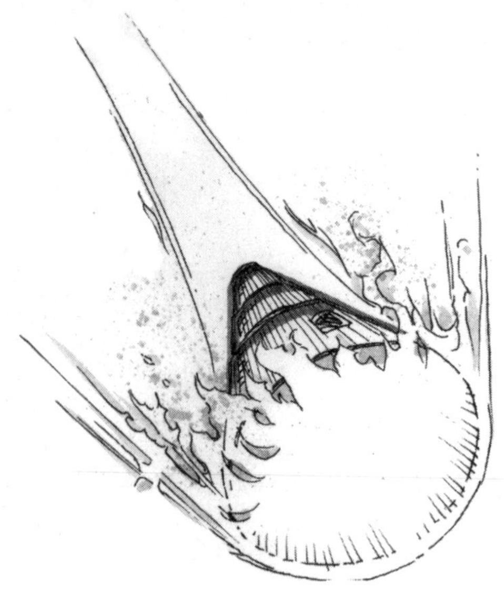